Using the Enneagram to Create Characters That Are Believable and Compelling

Using the Enneagram to Create Characters That Are Believable and Compelling

A Writer's Resource

By

Daniel A Taylor

Table of Contents

Intro

It has been said that a genius is not a person who knows everything. Rather, a genius is a person who knows how to find the answer to anything. This book will give you a non-AI resource that you can draw upon for all your basic character needs. My process is simple to understand, quick, and effortless. In no time, you will be creating like a pro.

Specifically, I will show you how to use the enneagram—a tool that has stood the test of time—to create characters who are believable, deep, and real. This tool is just as effective for heroes, sidekicks, friends, and villains.

Why do we need compelling characters? A story is meaningless without a character that we care about. I have a book at home that was recommended by one of my first editors. It is called "Fiction is Folks," by Robert Newton Peck. The title says it all. A story is all about your character. With that said, let's begin.

Chapter 1 What is the Enneagram?

The enneagram is a tool that has roots going as far back as the ancient Greeks, Homer's Odessey in 800 BC, Pythagoras in 600 BC, and Plato in 450 BC. It is widely used today as a tool for helping people to understand their own identity, and to understand the people around them.

While there are several personality tests and tools out there for self-discovery, the Enneagram is simple to understand, and it focuses on motivation. This is sufficient for my needs, and probably for yours. If you want to know why people do the things they do, this is the tool for you. If you want additional tools to track down how a person will behave—what actions these kinds of people take—then I might recommend other personality tests and descriptions, like the sixteen personalities, which is popular among teens and students. Another resource that you might find helpful is the Big Five Personality Test.

For the purposes of this book, we will use the Enneagram.

How many types of people are there in the world? Nine? Sixteen? Five? The truth is, there are as many personality types as there are people. But there are generalities, or forms, that are far more common. The Enneagram divides the generalities into nine types. This is a simplification. You may call it profiling, or even stereotyping. But in the field of writing and creating, we are not trying to label anyone, or pigeonhole them with an irrefutable judgement. We are merely trying to create a believable character and decide what motivates them.

There are a host of Enneagram resources online. I like the simple ones, like Enneagram Wikipedia, and the Enneagram Institute. Just run a simple google search, and you will find a plethora. Any of the top-rated sites will do.

A caution. If you make the personality compulsion too strong, you run the risk of making your character seem flat. I.e., a character driven by one thing. To prevent this, make sure not to overdo it. Granted, there are plenty of heroes and villains who are obsessively compelled to follow a path, but don't make it too obvious. And don't outright say it. Remember the old mantra, show, don't tell. And for the sake of your career as a writer, don't lay it all out in a breach of narrator exposition.

OCD characters can be fun and believable. If you want an eye-opening experience, search online for any notable character from your favorite books and movies, and you will find many-a-diagram cataloging their flaws, weaknesses, personality types, and disorders. Try searching the Avengers and their personality types. Can you doubt that the writers used personality types to create these characters? Think through some of your favorite movies. As you consider your protagonists and villains, it will become obvious.

Naturally, at some point in the adventure tell the backstory. It is important for the reader to understand *how they got that way*. It isn't unusual for a movie or book to start out with that backstory. It might be a fear of bats. Perhaps your hero's parents were killed by an evil wizard. Even normalcy can be a backstory. Your story begins in a hole in the ground, where your hero takes pride in being normal and never having adventures.

All of our Marvel characters have serious personality flaws. These flaws are there for a reason. No one wants to read a story about a perfect hero who does everything right a hundred percent of the time. A hero must have flaws, and they must make mistakes. Their personality traits and backstory drive these flaws and mistakes, and it is the overcoming—despite the flaws and mistakes—that makes the story interesting.

You might find it an interesting sidenote that a few of each personality type can sometimes be just as motivated by *being* the quality that describes their underlying motivation, as *appearing* to embrace that quality. It is how they perceive that society places value in them. For instance, a 7 sees their value to society being derived by others esteeming them to "be" fun. Which may drive that individual to "have" as much fun as possible, or to be esteemed by others as having fun. It's the difference between those who go riding ATVs without a camera, who go for the pure pleasure of it, and those who wouldn't make the trip without their camera, because their goal is not the experience, but merely to *look like* they had fun. Is their motivation to *have* fun? Or is it to *appear* to have fun, so that others will perceive them as fun.

From a distance, both individuals could be 7s. Unless the person is the second example is only trying to impress a 7, or there is another hidden objective. As people often are, it can get complicated.

There are many aspects and exceptions to each type, as there are also *wings* that describe a person's tendency to have secondary or tertiary traits from the other types. To be clear and concise, and to give you a solid tool, I will only focus on their core motivations and fears. Again, the enneagram is concerned about "why" they do the things they do, where other personality types are more focused on "what" that type of person does, or is likely to do.

Chapter 2 The Nine Types

I'm going to give you a nutshell of the nine types, as clear and concise as possible. The Sixteen Types is too complex for our purposes, and the Big Five oversimplifies. This is a writing tool, not an exhaustive treatise. We will discover the driving motivation, a struggle, and the worst fear. For better understanding, I have added stark contrasts to each type and a few examples.

Core motivations

Core motivations define our drive, our deepest values, the underlying *why* that determines the decisions we make and how we will react to various stimulus and situations. The sum of the core motivations is that we all want to be loved, understood, appreciated, safe, successful, happy, and valuable. The moving parts of these motivations is the unique understanding of those goals, and how they can be reached. These motivations do not control us, but they are extremely helpful in understanding the people around us, our employees, our family, and the person we are selling widgets to.

Fears

"My fears do not define me." While that is true of some people, it is an exception. Knowing what someone fears most is extremely helpful in understanding them, helping them, and communicating with them.

Struggles

This is a helpful identifier, something the person would generally struggle with. Know anyone with similar struggles?

Type 1, reformer

<u>Core Motivation:</u> The reformer, sometimes called the perfectionist, is concerned about doing the right thing. They have a strong moral compass, and seek to be virtuous, just, and good, or to be perceived as such. This drives their self-worth, and is how they see themselves being valuable to society.

<u>Fear:</u> Corruption. They will avoid breaking rules, or anything that could make them appear evil or corrupt.

<u>Struggle:</u> Refraining from pointing out errors and flaws in themselves and others. They just can't help it.

<u>Heaven:</u> For heaven to be heaven, it would be a place of truth, purity, justice, and righteousness. God is God because he is perfect, never lies, and never sins.

<u>Hell:</u> A place of deceitfulness, infidelity, corruption, and lawlessness, where no one obeys the rules.

<u>Examples:</u> Lisa Simpson, Moana, Queen Elinor (Brave), Cogsworth, Captain America, Yoda, CS Lewis, Mahatma Ghandi

Type 2, Helper

<u>Core Motivation:</u> The helper derives their self-value from helping others, or being perceived as helpful. They genuinely

want to serve, and they want to be useful. Their value is tied to being accommodating and serviceable.

<u>Fear:</u> Being unwanted.

<u>Struggle:</u> Letting a child learn from their mistake without intervening.

<u>Heaven:</u> A place where everyone is eager to help each other. God is God because He loves all of His children with a perfect love, and He will never stop helping them.

<u>Hell:</u> Where everyone cares and fends only for themselves, and no one is willing to help.

<u>Examples:</u> Fix-it Felix, Fairy Godmother (Cinderella), Anna (Frozen), Little John (Robin Hood, cartoon version), Black Panther, Hagrid (Harry Potter)

Type 3, Achiever

<u>Core Motivation:</u> Being the best, achieving highly, and being successful.

<u>Fear:</u> failure and mediocrity, being average, or less than average.

<u>Struggle:</u> Letting someone else win.

<u>Heaven:</u> A place where everyone sees you as supremely capable and successful. God is God because He is all powerful.

<u>Hell:</u> A place where everyone looks down on you for your inability to measure up.

<u>Examples:</u> Gaston, Hercules, Lightning McQueen (cars), Syndrome, Tiana, Tony Stark, Darth Vader, Buzz lightyear, Jafar, Randall (Monsters Inc), King Candy-Turbo (Wreck-it Ralph), Arnold Schwarzenegger

Type 4, Individualist

<u>Core Motivation:</u> Being unique, different from the crowd.

<u>Fear:</u> Being common, having nothing different to set them apart.

<u>Struggle:</u> Conforming to an assignment that requires them to produce the exact same object or result as everyone else.

<u>Heaven:</u> Being understood and appreciated for their unique contributions that only they can bring. God is God because no one else is like Him, and no one else can do what He does.

<u>Hell:</u> Being the same as everyone else, and not having anything unique to contribute.

<u>Examples:</u> Belle, Remy (Ratatouille), Flik (Bug's Life), Doctor Strange, Kylo Ren (Star Wars), Johnny Depp, Billie Eilish, Luna Lovegood (Harry Potter), Edgar Allen Poe

Type 5, Investigator

<u>Core Motivation:</u> Knowledge. To understand. Their value is derived from acquiring knowledge that can help them and others navigate the world.

<u>Fear:</u> Being hurt or disadvantaged by the unknown.

<u>Heaven:</u> A place of wisdom and understanding where there is nothing that is not known. God is God because he is all knowing.

<u>Hell:</u> A place of darkness, full of uncertainty and doubt.

<u>Examples:</u> Jane (Tarzan), Ender Wiggin (Ender's Game, the book, not the movie), Dr. Jumba (Lilo and Stitch), Merlin (Sword in the Stone), Lewis (Meet the Robinsons), Sherlock Holmes, Dr. Frankenstein (not the monster), Dr. Octavius (Spiderman), Albert Einstein

Type 6, Loyalist

<u>Core Motivation:</u> Support from family connections and relationships.

<u>Fear:</u> Getting stranded and being alone, without support.

<u>Struggle:</u> Going solo on a trip far from friend and home.

<u>Heaven:</u> A place where everyone loves and cares about you, and all support each other. God is God because He will never let you down.

<u>Hell:</u> A place where no one cares about you.

<u>Examples:</u> Bolt, Mulan, Hawkeye, Homer Simpson (with a type 7 wing), Tarzan, Frankenstein's Monster, Marlin and Dory (Finding Nemo), Rapunzel (Tangled), Woody (Toy Story), Carl Fredricksen (Up), Stitch (Lilo and Stitch), JRR Tolkien

Type 7, Enthusiast

Core Motivation: Fun and excitement. They live for exhilaration.

Fear: Boredom and monotony. Dull tedium is pain. Life is drab and flavorless without the color and spice of excitement.

Struggle: Quietly sitting through a dull lecture.

Heaven: A place of excitement and newness of life. God is God because there is no limit to his enjoyment, and He is perfectly happy, having no end to the pleasures that he has access to.

Hell: A place that lacks the luster of joy and pleasure. Boring school classes and a tedious nine-to-five job are the stuff of nightmares for 7s.

Examples: Emperor Kuzco, Jack Skellington (The Nightmare Before Christmas), Bart Simpson (with a type 8 wing), Ariel, Genie (Aladdin), Olaf (Frozen), Ellie and Dug (Up), Lilo Pelekai (Lilo and Stitch), Mushu (Mulan), Flynn Rider (Tangled), Venellope Von Schweetz (Wreck-it Ralph)

Type 8, Challenger

Core Motivation: Freedom. "The Resistance." To protect themselves and others from being used, deceived, and controlled by those would enslave and exploit.

Fear: Being controlled by anyone or anything, including rules and social constructions.

Struggle: Bowing to authority or obeying a law they think is stupid.

Heaven: A place of complete freedom where no one will ever try to control or harm you. God is God because He has ultimate freedom to do anything, and no one can constrain Him.

Hell: A place of captivity, where everyone is bound to follow rules that are constructed to cause pain and slavery.

Examples: Jasmine (Aladdin), Leia (Star Wars), Merida (Brave), Maximus (Gladiator), Jack Sparrow, Robin Hood, Zoro, The Scarlet Pimpernel

Type 9, Peacemaker

Core Motivation: Peace. They want the world and themselves to be at peace. "Can't everyone just get along?"

Fear: Confrontation and conflict. They will do anything to avoid being the cause of disruption.

Struggle: Taking a stand or calling someone out.

Heaven: A place of peace, where people are perfectly obedient to a higher law. There is no fighting, squabbling, or contention. God is God because he is the essence of peace and love.

Hell: A place of contention, lawlessness, and hatred.

Examples: Kronk (Emperor's New Groove), Marge Simpson (with a type 1 wing), Cinderella, Kristoff (Frozen), Quasimodo (Hunchback of Notre dame)

Chapter 3 Wings

It is more common than not for a person to have another sub-dominant personality type. These are called "wings," which are usually adjacent to the personality type on both sides. Technically, a personality has two adjacent wings, but one will be much stronger than the other.

Lisa Simpson, for example, is a strong type 1 Reformer. She values doing the right thing. For her, it is a high enough priority that it often brings her into conflict with her brother and her father, who both disregard rules with wild abandon.

But she also tends to be a strong 2 Helper, as a sub-dominant wing, especially when it comes to getting her family out of trouble.

The writers of Simpsons have done a remarkable job staying true to their character's values and motivations. But they are writers, and their characters are works of fiction. Occasionally you catch the Simpsons going against their dominant compass. Real people are not so different, and can be persuaded to sail on a different wind. They may even surprise you on their own, without needing any persuasion. But these cases are the exception, not the rule.

Let's look at the rest of the family. Marge is a type 9 Peacemaker, with a type 1 Reformer wing. She is constantly mediating conflict in the home and keeping the family together. But she will try to persuade them to do the right thing. Because she places a lot of value on morals, she is often pushed out of her comfort zone on dealing with Homer. Thus, she is conflicted, torn between being loving, accepting, and peaceful—and doing the right thing by going against her husband. In many an episode, Marge can be seen pressing her lips together as she grinds out her frustration. She wants to do the right thing, but she doesn't want to be in conflict with Homer.

Homer is also a type 9 peacemaker, but he's a lazy one. And he has a type 8 Challenger wing. Homer will take whatever side of an argument keeps him out of conflict, and will easily lie to push that conflict away. His challenger side is less dominant, but it is there. He doesn't like all the socially acceptable rules of being honest and hard-working. He bucks the system that says he needs to be on the pious treadmill of life. He outright rebels against every code of health and fitness, willing to risk disease, obesity, and reputational damage for a constant intake of donuts, beer, and laziness.

Lastly, we come to Bart, a true personality type 8 Challenger, with a type 7 Enthusiast subtype wing. When it comes to school, church, and being socially acceptable, Bart isn't just tardy, he's a no show. A constant Loki and a prankster, he would cheat his way through school, church, and chores without a second thought. His thoughts are on the arcade, mischief, and adventure, willing to leap in with both feet. Yes, sometimes his conscience injects enough guilt to compel him to right a wrong, but the mistake was initially made without thought of remorse. Bart's moments of guilt are, on one hand, incriminating, while on the other hand, they make him redeemable and relatable. There is some good in Bart, and that's why we still love him.

Oh, you wanted to know about Maggie? Well... she's observant, innocent, thoughtful, and is generally easy going. I'm basing my best guess on what she isn't, rather than what she is. She isn't a disrupter or a fighter. You rarely, if ever, see or hear her cry. There is no malice in those eyes of hers. She isn't out to challenge or outshine. Because she never wanders off to explore the world—she is given ample opportunity—I suppose she could be a type 6 Loyalist, with a faithfulness that ties her to her family. However, I would place her in the

9 Peacemaker category with a 1 Reformer wing. She is peaceful and law abiding.

More

For more details, just search "enneagram," or the "nine types," in Google, and you will find a feast of information. There are also plenty of books on Audible or Kindle that are fun and informative. If you want to go beyond motivation and make a study of behavior, try one of the other tests like the 16 personality types. Again, just do a search.

Chapter 4 Character Sheets

Character sheets are important because they keep track of important details. If you're anything like me, your story will flourish with action, adventure, magic, and a bit of humor and romance. In all of the commotion and mix of characters, it can be easy to forget a simple detail, like what type of shirt they are wearing, or what color their eyes are. Trust me, and set up a character sheet. It will save you a lot of catch-up time when you get to book four.

My own books

The following character sheets are characters that I have created for my own series, Legends of Pangea. So far, I have 4 books, "Awakening," "Refiner's Fire," "XP Farming," and "Starforged." It will be a 9 book series when I'm done with it.

You can download my Character Sheet Template on my website, legendsofpangea.com .

I added the images using a free online program called Playground, which uses AI to generate images based on the prompts you enter. The images are a generic "this is generally what they look like," kind of accuracy. It's super easy. I generated most of these on my first try. See the following page for an example of a character sheet template.

A special note on "Heart's Desire." This is a phrase and concept pioneered by author Wulf Moon. I agree fully with the concept. It is indispensable to an effective story. His book, "How to Write a Howling Good Story," is one of the best that I have read on the subject of writing.

Using the Enneagram to Create Characters That Are
Believable and Compelling

Name:
Age:
Hair:
Eyes:
Body Style:
Clothing, Glasses, etc:
Weapon, or something they carry around:
Personality Type: Enneagram type(s)
Heart's Desire: What do they want more than anything else?
Strength: Can be anything. Go Generic or be unique.
Talent: Unique ability that applies to my Age of Magic.
Fears: What are they afraid of?
Value to Others: What makes others care about and need them?
Weakness: Every hero needs at least one.
Handicap: Don't make it easy.
Character Flaws: Make them human.
Self-doubts: Insecurities are a part of life.
Backstory: Partially explains why they do the things they do.
Secrets: Don't leave home without at least one.
Unique words they use: Make sure your characters don't share the same "voice."
Unique gestures: "They should be unique."
Things they love and build their paradigm around: What makes them happy?
Unique lens, the way they see the world: Keep this in mind while writing.
Pet Peeve: Something that irritates them, can set them off.

Example Character Sheets:

Consider the following examples.

Name: Enoch Arthur Anderson
Age: 14
Hair: Black
Eyes: Dark Brown
Body Style: Slender. Not athletic. Shorter than average. Later he is observed as "less scrawny." As the story progresses, he becomes athletic and muscular.
Clothing, Glasses, etc: Usually black, baggy, looking slept in, giving an "I don't care," vibe.
Weapon, or something they carry around: Ring of Gortax
Personality Type: Enneagram type 8 Challenger, with a type 7 Enthusiast wing. Quiet and introverted, Enoch doesn't agree with the expectations constructed by society. His parents promote choosing a passion early in life, so their children can thrive, being useful to society. Enoch wants nothing to do with society. He avoids people, and would rather be gaming online.
Heart's Desire: Not to be controlled by school, family, or a 9-5 job. He would rather be online, taking on a boss in a dungeon.
Strength: Independent. Doesn't bow to others. Doesn't need to follow the rules. Strictly avoids anything addictive or controlling. Learns important traits from video games, like never giving up, and getting stronger through effort and leveling up.
Talent: Dream Thief. He can steal things from his dreams, and see things and events from the past, present, and future. His talent remains undeveloped and misunderstood, because he has all the abilities of the Infinity Knights within him. When he's connected with the Infinity Knights, he is unstoppable.

<u>Fears:</u> That he is Gortax. Being controlled by stupid rules. That his family will never get back together. That he will never live down his past. That he will disappoint his friends and family.

<u>Value to Others:</u> As an 8, he sees himself as valuable to others if he can provide a perspective that can help others survive and dwell together in freedom and peace. He isn't afraid of being different.

<u>Weakness:</u> Doesn't care for reputation, rules, or social propriety. Others see him as lazy and indifferent, which isn't wrong.

<u>Handicap:</u> He thinks he is Gortax, so he must pursue his kidnapped wife and daughter. People he grew up with see him as a bad kid. He got off on the wrong foot with Hayven. They see each other as enemies.

<u>Character Flaws:</u> Standoffish. He can be blunt.

<u>Self-doubts:</u> Doesn't think he should be leading anyone, so he shrugs off the mantle that he should be carrying.

<u>Backstory:</u> He idolizes Jed, who is a master persuader and communicator. He lives for video games and strategy—not necessarily to win, but to surprise and upset. He also loves problem solving.

<u>Secrets:</u> Thinks he killed his dad by sneaking him cookies while he was in the hospital. His identity as Gortax, and his association with Morgana.

<u>Unique words they use:</u> Blunt and to the point. Often, he will say nothing.

<u>Unique gestures:</u> Folds his arms. Looks away. Indifference.

<u>Things they love and build their paradigm around:</u> By caring for Aja, Family becomes very important to Enoch. Helping the world find an easier and better way also becomes important. Protecting others and preventing wars becomes a huge priority as the story unfolds.

<u>Unique lens, the way they see the world:</u> Videogame mentality. Not quitting. Leveling up through effort and experience.

<u>Pet Peeve:</u> People who want to control others.

Name: Jacob Fergus Williams
Age: 14
Hair: Sandy Blond, with a hint of Red
Eyes: Blue
Body style: Athletic / Slender
Clothing, glasses, etc: Nothing fancy, but clean. Usually a T-shirt, blue jeans, tennis shoes.
Weapon, or something they carry around: Thuban, the obsidian sabers of Draco.
Personality Type: Reformer, Enneagram 1, with a 9 Peacemaker wing. He has a keen sense of right and wrong. Everything is black and white, with very little gray area. In school, he was made fun of because of his love for obeying rules and being "good" on a scale that his peers could never understand. His friendship with Enoch softened that reputation. Being peaceful is an important part of being good. His tolerance of others must be abandoned when he becomes a church knight. But can he also be merciful? It will be an inner conflict as the story progresses.
Heart's Desire: Justice and Righteousness. To do the right thing. To be good.
Strength: Honesty, Keeping Commitments.
Talent: Platypus powers, sees in the dark and in murky water, strength in water, can hold breath, poison spurs. (he keeps all of these secret.)
Fears: Doing the wrong thing, giving in to temptation.
Value to others: His value is derived from others perceiving him as worthy and pure
Weakness: He puts honesty and justice before his friends, especially Hayley
Handicap: Tone deaf. He loves Hayley, but can't show it because it wouldn't be right. His parents hurt him a lot physically when he was a child. Physical and Verbal abuse.

<u>Character Flaws:</u> Has an overdeveloped sense of justice and doesn't see anything wrong with punishing those who do evil. He perceives that they will hurt others, and must be dealt with.

<u>Self-doubts:</u> He is painfully aware of his own imperfections and temptations. He isn't perfect, and that hurts. He likes Hayley, but doesn't think he should. Wants to be obedient to a rule of not seriously dating anyone before he is 16. He goes out of his way to avoid being seen as in love with her.

<u>Backstory:</u> Abusive parents. Jacob had to cover up a lot of injuries inflicted by his parents by saying he was unlucky. He loved a tv program on the platypus. Says his luck has changed with the TOA.

<u>Secrets:</u> Says he is lucky. It is a half-truth to cover up his platypus powers, which is an embarrassment for him.

<u>Unique words they use:</u> "Curiouser." "Indeed." Often thoughtful, thinking before speaking, but prioritizing what it right.

<u>Unique gestures:</u> Rubs his chin.

<u>Things they love and build their paradigm around:</u> Warrior of light. Defender of truth and justice. He becomes a Church Knight. He can find the good, like in the R-rated movies he was exposed to, but he doesn't ignore—or forgive—the bad.

<u>Unique lens, the way they see the world:</u> Doing what is right. Following the rules. If everyone would just follow the rules and choose kindness and righteousness, the world would be an amazing place.

<u>Pet Peeve:</u> Hates people who break the rules and disregard laws. As the story progresses, he becomes less and less tolerant of those who turn a blind eye to evil.

<u>Name:</u> Aja Lucille Anderson
<u>Age:</u> 10
<u>Hair:</u> Sandy Blond
<u>Eyes:</u> Blue-green
<u>Body Style:</u> Small
<u>Clothing, Glasses, etc:</u> Usually green, later becoming sprite-like, with leaves and vines.
<u>Weapon, or something they carry around:</u> Her cat, Mr. Wigglemittens.

As an Ally of Nature, she has a unique bond with her cat that lets her communicate with him. Mr. Wigglemittens can grow in size, becoming as large as a powerful horse. Aja rides him with an agile grace.

<u>Personality Type:</u> Enneagram 9, peacemaker, quiet, loves all things nature. She loves to draw plants and animals.
<u>Heart's Desire:</u> To get her family back. Peace. Hence she hates Enoch.
<u>Strength:</u> Independent, empathetic,
<u>Talent:</u> Growing magic. Nature's Ally. Her cat, Mr. Wigglemittens, grows as large as a horse.
<u>Fears:</u> Conflict, confrontation, chaos.
<u>Value to Others:</u> As a promoter of peace, she sees that others would value her as a shade-giving tree. She is an anchor in the storm. A protector and a provider. Often a mediator and advocate, except in Enoch's case. She eventually grows to care deeply for Enoch.
<u>Weakness:</u> Shyness. She will act out in times of crisis.
<u>Handicap:</u> She's young, small, and timid.
<u>Character Flaws:</u> Doesn't like Enoch. Misses her family a lot.
<u>Self-doubts:</u> That she can't help the world find peace.
<u>Backstory:</u> Grew up in the Anderson home where Enoch was always a jerk to everyone. She loves nature and her cat.

<u>Secrets:</u> She has a little-girl crush on Jacob, and can be defensive of him, and a little mean to Hayley.

<u>Unique words they use:</u> Few words. Quietness. Hard working.

<u>Unique gestures:</u> Escaping to be by herself or with her cat.

<u>Things they love and build their paradigm around:</u> Nature, her cat, plants, animals.

<u>Unique lens, the way they see the world:</u> Nature. Everyone should get along.

<u>Pet Peeve:</u> Angry people

<u>Name:</u> Hayley McGee
<u>Age:</u> 14
<u>Hair:</u> Red
<u>Eyes:</u> Brown
<u>Body Style:</u> Average. Not slender or athletic. Not stocky or overweight. Not tall or short.
<u>Clothing, Glasses, etc:</u> T-shirt, jeans, sneakers. Simple and clean.
<u>Weapon, or something they carry around:</u> Diamond Pendant

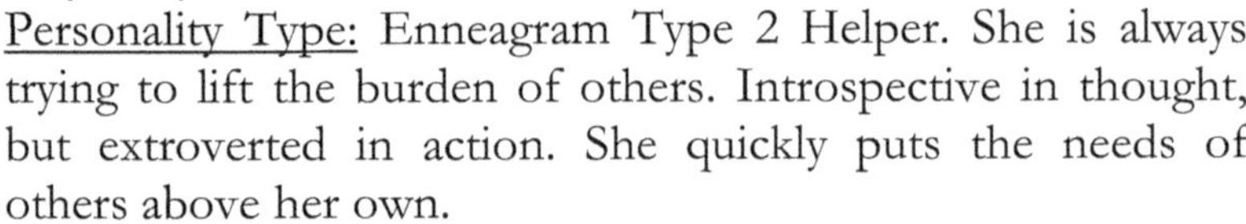

<u>Personality Type:</u> Enneagram Type 2 Helper. She is always trying to lift the burden of others. Introspective in thought, but extroverted in action. She quickly puts the needs of others above her own.

<u>Heart's Desire:</u> To help her family by finding Hayden. To help her new friends who helped her. As story progresses, she wants to help the world.

<u>Strength:</u> Altruism. Unselfish.

<u>Talent:</u> Conditional Magic. Lifting, elevating, changing the gravity of an object.

<u>Fears:</u> That her sister will fail because she wasn't helpful enough. /that she will let others down.

<u>Value to Others:</u> In helping them. She sees that she has value to others because she is helpful.

<u>Weakness:</u> Always puts herself last. She makes sure everyone else's needs are met first. This can leave her tired and burnt out.

<u>Handicap:</u> Perceived need to help her sister

<u>Character Flaws:</u> too kind. Thinks that she has to protect her older sister.

<u>Self-doubts:</u> Not sure if others like her. Although he says otherwise, she worries that Jacob doesn't love her. He never shows it.

<u>Backstory:</u> Raised by her mother in a broken family.

<u>Secrets:</u> She likes Enoch, but she hides this secret, even from herself because Hayven likes him. She publicly likes Jacob, and wants to like him.

<u>Unique words they use:</u> uplifting words, rarely if ever negative. Quietly optimistic.

<u>Unique gestures:</u> twirls her pendant. Lifts her hand as if lifting the person she talks to.

<u>Things they love and build their paradigm around:</u> Light, family, lifting burdens.

<u>Unique lens, the way they see the world:</u> Supporting and helping others

<u>Pet Peeve:</u> Those who take without giving back, people who litter.

<u>Name:</u> Hayven McGee
<u>Age:</u> 16
<u>Hair:</u> Red
<u>Eyes:</u> Brown
<u>Body Style:</u> Athletic
<u>Clothing, Glasses, etc:</u> T-shirt. Blue Jeans. Tennis shoes
<u>Weapon, or something they carry around:</u> Diamond Pendant
<u>Personality Type:</u>

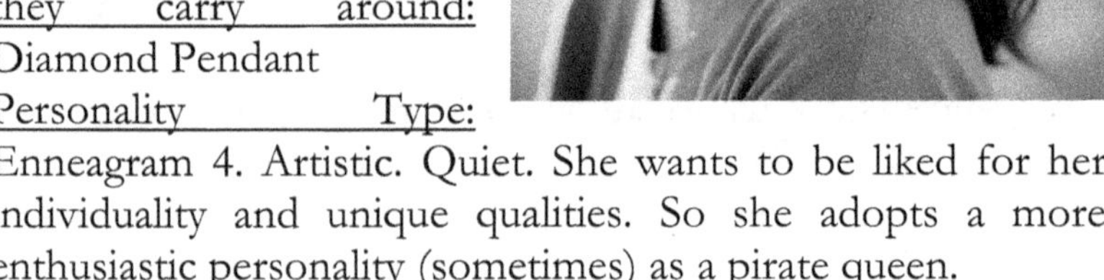

Enneagram 4. Artistic. Quiet. She wants to be liked for her individuality and unique qualities. So she adopts a more enthusiastic personality (sometimes) as a pirate queen.
<u>Heart's Desire:</u> To be understood, loved, and accepted.
<u>Strength:</u> Willing to step out of her comfort zone.
<u>Talent:</u> Conditional Magic. Light. She can make things light up when surrounded by darkness.
<u>Fears:</u> Of being like everyone else. Stepping out of her comfort zone, into the unknown. The Dark.
<u>Value to Others:</u> In bringing her unique perspective to the world. Bringing light.
<u>Weakness:</u> Afraid of the dark.
<u>Handicap:</u> Fear paralysis. Afraid that people will not like her. Impulsive
<u>Character Flaws:</u> Violent temper.
<u>Self-doubts:</u> They will never see their mom again. Worries that Hayley is always sticking up for her and protecting her.
<u>Backstory:</u> Mistreated by her father, Hayven has been beaten into quiet submission. She never talks about it. When she tries, she locks up.
<u>Secrets:</u> Physical abuse in her past as a child. Fear of the dark. Crush on Enoch.
<u>Unique words they use:</u> Pirate words. Sailor speech. Uses ocean and ship imagery to describe things and communicate.

Unique gestures: Rolling her eyes. Smug frown. Looking
small
Things they love and build their paradigm around: Family,
light, freedom.
Unique lens, the way they see the world: Skepticism. Takes
time for her to trust.
Pet Peeve: Those who would take advantage of her and her
friends.

<u>Name:</u> Aximus
<u>Age:</u> 34
<u>Hair:</u> Brown
<u>Eyes:</u> Blue
<u>Body Style:</u> Massive, wrestler, white teeth
<u>Clothing, Glasses, etc:</u> Hooded Cloak
<u>Weapon, or something they carry around:</u> Soul Stones
<u>Personality Type:</u> Enneagram type 1. Reformer.
<u>Heart's Desire:</u> Redemption. Forgiveness.
<u>Strength:</u> Protecting Others
<u>Talent:</u> Energy reserve. He doesn't get fatigued. Soul stone lets him see a few seconds into the future.
<u>Fears:</u> His Past.
<u>Value to Others:</u> Protects others, especially children, and those who are unable to protect themselves. Hero.
<u>Weakness:</u> He has a bit of a death wish. Despite trying the rest of his life, he doesn't think he can compensate for the crime of his past. Heavy handed on those he perceives as evil.
<u>Handicap:</u> Labeled with evil. His old friends, Onai and Okem are after him for revenge.
<u>Character Flaws:</u> He can have a very black and white perspective. He doesn't hesitate to try to kill Enoch when he thinks he is Gortax.
<u>Self-doubts:</u> Being unworthy. Also being unworthy of his friend, Anathema.
<u>Backstory:</u> He had a very bad childhood that led to bad decisions as a youth and young man.
<u>Secrets:</u> He killed his old girlfriend on her wedding night, when she was marrying his best friend, and he was high on drugs. He doesn't remember the event, but police reports painted him in a very bad light.

<u>Unique words they use:</u> Shot at redemption phrases, a strong sense of self-sacrifice.
<u>Unique gestures:</u> Flexing his jaw, flexing in general.
<u>Things they love and build their paradigm around:</u> Friends, the cause, people who embrace the cause. Protecting children.
<u>Unique lens, the way they see the world:</u> Justice and protecting the innocent.
<u>Pet Peeve:</u> Flippant and mocking idiots.

My Characters

Enoch is the hero of this story. He detests all the rules and social expectations heaped on him by society. He believes there is a better way, but he doesn't want to be the one to initiate change. An editor once remarked to me that she absolutely hated Enoch's character. "Well done," she said.

Jacob is a reformer and peacemaker who innately follows rules. He doesn't understand why anyone would want to break a rule.

Enoch and Jacob are best friends. As you could probably guess, Enoch's disregard for rules will often conflict with Jacob's need to follow them.

Hayley and Hayven are sisters. Hayley is a natural helper who lifts the burdens of others. Hayven is more of an uncertain character. She is usually quiet and struggles to express herself.

Aja is Enoch's little sister. She loves peace. Naturally, she hates Enoch's disruptive and indifferent nature. As Enoch and Aja are separated from their family, Enoch's perspective is completely changed as he tries to protect and care for her.

Aximus needs a shot at redemption. He has made choices that have hurt other people, and he is doing everything he can to atone for his crimes.

Chapter 5 Don't Neglect Your Inner Villain

"In spite of everything I still believe that people are really good at heart. I simply can't build up my hopes on a foundation consisting of confusion, misery, and death."
~ Diary of Anne Frank, Jewish holocaust survivor

Not all villains are created equal. Some of the best villains in all literature weren't evil—they were motivated by good.

Megatron wanted to save his planet. Are you with me on this one? Megatron and Optimus fought together against a corrupt government. Then Optimus takes the one thing that keeps their entire planet alive, and chucks it through a portal. Megatron wants to bring it back to save the planet. While Optimus champions all life in the universe, what about the planet he doomed by taking the AllSpark?

If Ahsoka had listened to Darth Maul, they may have prevented the rise of Palpatine and the Empire.

Killmonger believed that Wakanda should share its technology with a suffering world.

Doctor Doom only wanted his mother back.

Thanos, the villain who annihilated half the people in the universe, was trying to protect it from the celestials and solve an overpopulation problem.

Sandman wanted to help his ailing daughter.

Syndrome initially wanted to fight crime like Mr. Incredible. Shunned, he wanted equality for non-supers, and respect.

Magneto wanted equality for mutants.

Lord Beckett, from the Pirates of the Caribbean stories, wanted to purge the world of piracy.

What ultimately twisted these virtues into evil, was their methods. The ends do not justify the means. Their methods were often brutal and merciless. I mean, look at the last example. Ridding the world of piracy seems like a pretty noble aspiration. But are the brutalities justified?

Anyway, the whole point of this section is that you can use the same tools above to forge great villains. They are still people. They have a heart, just like you and me. And they have their motivations, quirks, mothers, and backstories.

Chapter 6 One More Tool

Before I go, I wanted to leave you with one more goldmine. If you really need help creating a character, use a second-hand creation. Find any character from any book or movie that you love, and give them a different name, physical appearance, and backstory. For example, I really like Sam from Lord of the Rings. For my second-hand character, I'm going to make him a mouse, and say that he was bullied in his childhood. Second-hand charactering is amazingly easy, and is great for beginners. This is true for a number of reasons. First, it helps so your character isn't a blank sheet. A blank page can be overwhelming. Second, you can hear their unique voice in your mind's ear.

Remember, this is a tool of creation, not imitation. Do not copy their exact words or actions, as that opens you up to lawsuits for plagiarism and may very well get you flogged by your readers. It's about the heart of the character and their voice. Perhaps take the character you love and find a way to make them the villain. Imagine how that character would respond, how they would feel, what general kinds of words they would use, and what would be their heart's desire.

Conclusion

I hope you have fun with this tool, and I know it will help you develop realistic and believable characters that people will love (or hate, depending on your objective).